DEC 0 7

1/11-4

# WORLD OF INSECTS

# Mosquitoes

by Martha E. H. Rustad

GLEN ELLYN PUBLIC LIBRARY
400 DUANE STREET
GLEN ELLYN, ILLINOIS 60137

BLASTOFF!
READERS
2

BELLWETHER MEDIA • MINNEAPOLIS, MN

Note to Librarians, Teachers, and Parents:

**Blastoff! Readers** are carefully developed by literacy experts and combine standards-based content with developmentally-appropriate text.

**Level 1** provides the most support through repetition of high-frequency words, light text, predictable sentence patterns, and strong visual support.

**Level 2** offers early readers a bit more challenge through varied simple sentences, increased text load, and less repetition of high frequency words.

**Level 3** advances early-fluent readers toward fluency through increased text and concept load, less reliance on visuals, longer sentences, and more literary language.

**Level 4** builds reading stamina by providing more text per page, increased use of punctuation, greater variation in sentence patterns, and increasingly challenging vocabulary.

**Level 5** encourages children to move from "learning to read" to "reading to learn" by providing even more text, varied writing styles, and less familiar topics.

Whichever book is right for your reader, Blastoff! Readers are the perfect books to build confidence and encourage a love of reading that will last a lifetime!

This edition first published in 2008 by Bellwether Media.

No part of this publication may be reproduced in whole or in part without written permission of the publisher. For information regarding permission, write to Bellwether Media Inc., Attention: Permissions Department, Post Office Box 1C, Minnetonka, MN 55345-9998.

Library of Congress Cataloging-in-Publication Data
Rustad, Martha E. H. (Martha Elizabeth Hillman), 1975–
  Mosquitoes / by Martha E.H. Rustad.
    p. cm. – (Blastoff! readers. World of insects)
Summary: "Simple text accompanied by full-color photographs give an upclose look at mosquitoes. Intended for kindergarten through third grade students"–Provided by publisher.
  Includes bibliographical references and index.
  ISBN-13: 978-1-60014-078-5 (hardcover : alk. paper)
  ISBN-10: 1-60014-078-5 (hardcover : alk. paper)
  1. Mosquitoes–Juvenile literature. I. Title.

QL536.R89 2008
595.77'2–dc22                                    2007009764

Text copyright © 2008 by Bellwether Media.
SCHOLASTIC, CHILDREN'S PRESS, and associated logos are trademarks and/or registered trademarks of Scholastic Inc. Printed in the United States of America.

# Contents

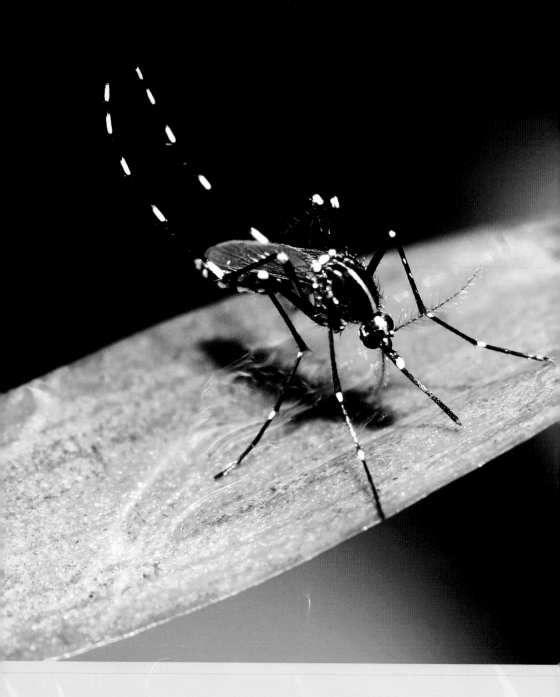

Mosquitoes are **insects**.

Mosquitoes buzz through the
air on warm nights.

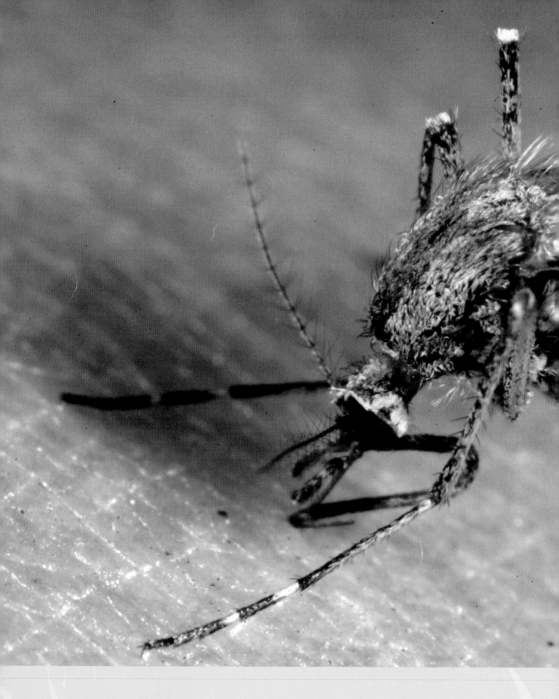

Mosquitoes have slim bodies. Most are gray, black, or brown.

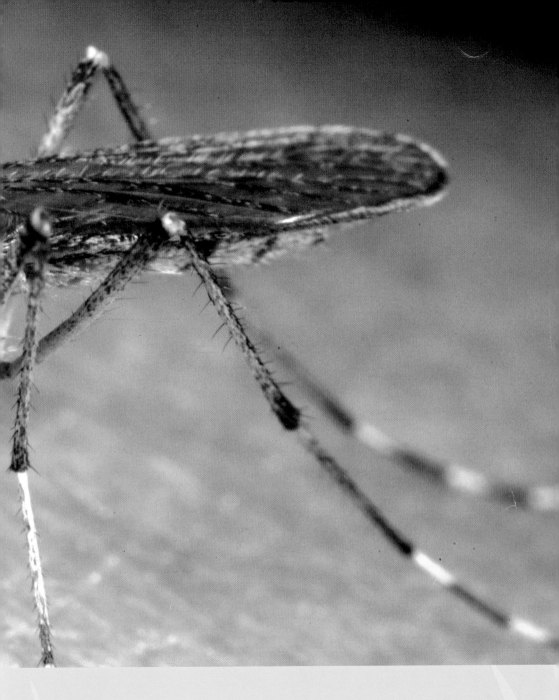

Some are more colorful.

Mosquitoes have two thin wings. **Scales** cover their wings.

8

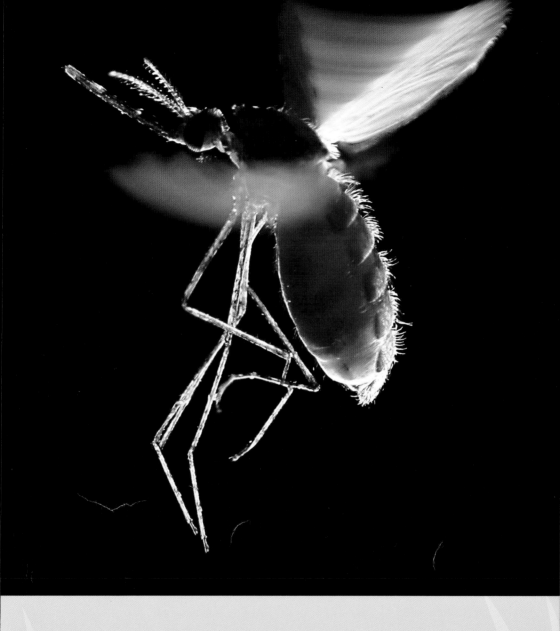

Mosquitoes move their wings quickly to fly. Moving wings make a buzzing sound.

9

Mosquitoes drink **nectar** from flowers. Nectar gives them energy for flying.

10

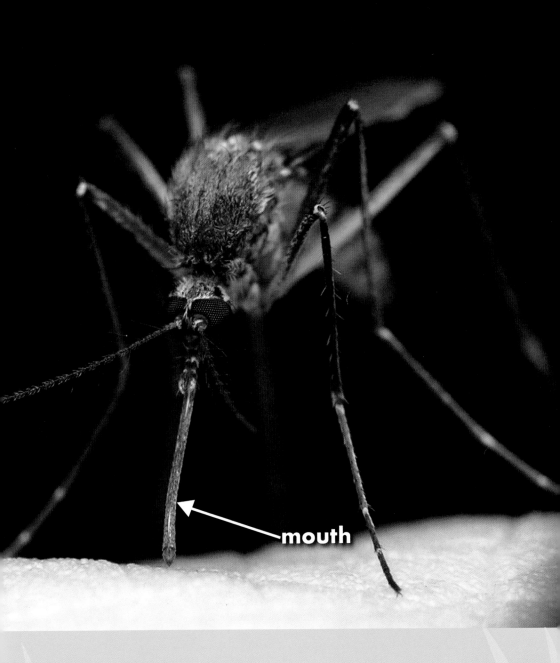

**mouth**

A mosquito's mouth is shaped like a straw. They drink nectar through it.

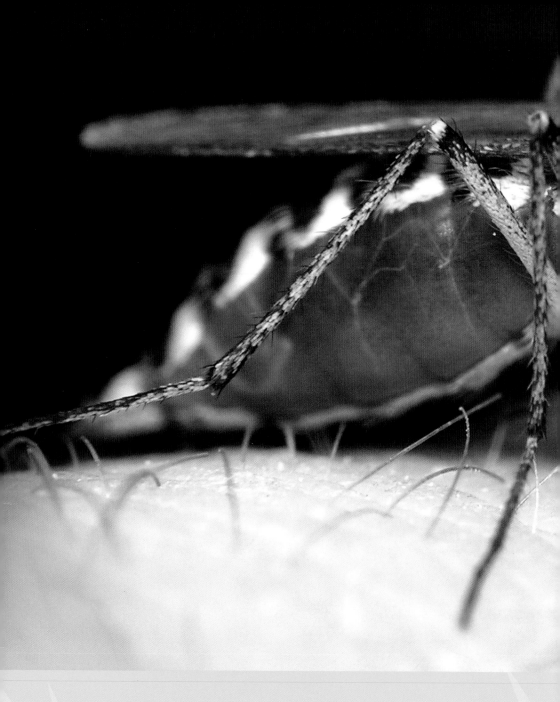

Female mosquitoes also drink blood. They need blood to grow eggs.

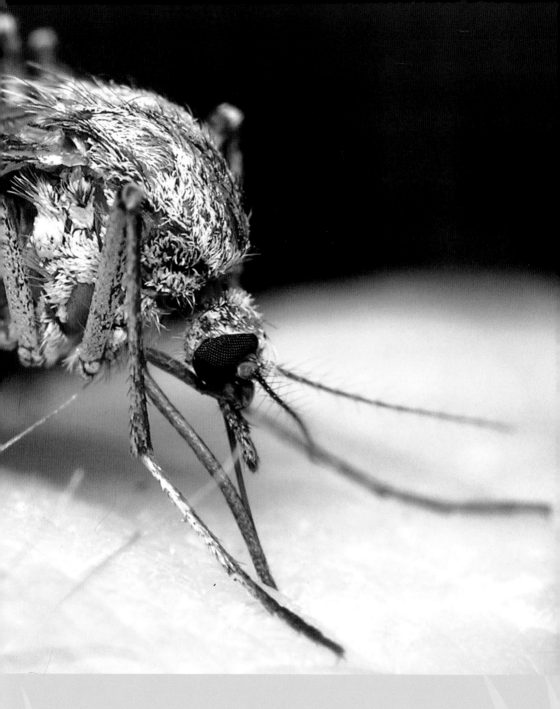

A female's mouth ends in two sharp points. They can poke through skin.

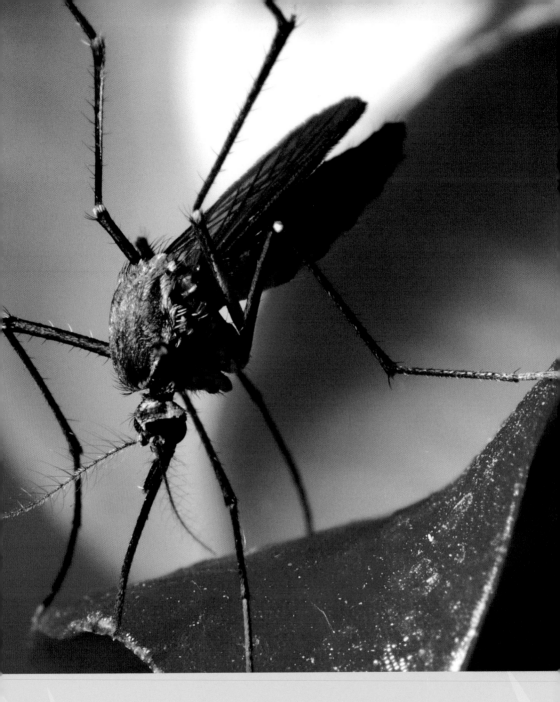

All insects have six legs.
Mosquitoes have a **claw**
at the end of each leg.

14

Claws help them grip
plants. They can even
land upside down!

Mosquitoes have two eyes.
But they do not see well.

Mosquito eyes only see
movement. This helps them
escape from danger!

antennas

Mosquitoes have two hairy **antennas**. They use their antennas to smell food.

18

Females follow the smell of people and animals to find blood.

Mosquito antennas also **sense** heat. This helps them find people and animals.

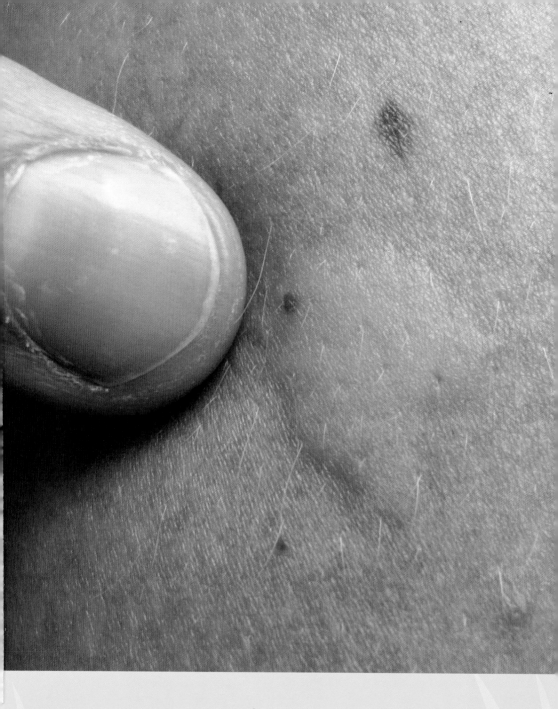

Mosquitoes bite! They leave
liquid in the skin that makes
you itch. Ouch!

# Glossary

**antennas**—a pair of thin feelers on an insect's head; mosquitoes use their antennas to feel and smell.

**claw**—a sharp hook on the leg of an insect

**insect**—a kind of animal with six legs; most insects also have a hard body, two antennas, and two or four wings.

**nectar**—sugary juice found in flowers

**scales**—small, hard plates that cover a body part of some insects and animals

**sense**—to become aware of something

# To Learn More

## AT THE LIBRARY

Birch, Robin. *Mosquitoes Up Close*. Chicago, Ill.: Raintree, 2005.

Jacobs, Liza. *Mosquitoes*. San Diego, Calif.: Blackbirch Press, 2003.

Kravetz, Jonathan. *Mosquitoes*. New York: PowerKids Press, 2006.

## ON THE WEB

Learning more about mosquitoes is as easy as 1, 2, 3.

1. Go to www.factsurfer.com

2. Enter "mosquitoes" into search box.

3. Click the "Surf" button and you will see a list of related web sites.

With factsurfer.com, finding more information is just a click away.

# Index

The photographs in this book are reproduced through the courtesy of: Wojciech Wojcik, front cover, pp. 6-7; Hugh Sturrock/Wellcome Photo Library, pp. 5, 9; Pham Thi Lan Anh, p. 4; R. Nagel/Peter Arnold, Inc, p. 8; Jim Brandenburg/Minden Pictures, p. 10; Yaroslav, pp. 11, 12-13; Pailoolom/Dreamstime.com, p. 14; Jeridu/Dreamstime.com, pp. 15, 18; Dwight Kuhn, pp. 16-17; Scott Camazine/Alamy, p. 19; Ron Chapple/Getty Images, p. 20; Simon Krzic, p. 21.